For Everything a Season

In Verse

Other Writings

The Homecoming and Other Stories

The Michael/Lucifer Correspondence

There are Animals in my Alphabet (verse)

BJ Bear and the Magical Ladybug

The Monster of Rainbow Outlook

A Dangerous Surprise

The Ghost of Willow Park

The Star of Bethlehem is Missing

For Everything a Season
In Verse

James W. Greig

A Dunbarton North Publication

2014

Copyright © 2014 by James W. Greig

Cataloguing in Publication

Greig, James W., 1930-, author
    For everything a season : in verse / James W. Greig.

Includes index.
Poems.
ISBN 978-0-9917351-1-2 (pbk.)

    I. Title.

PS8613.R447F67 2014   C811'.6   C2014-900862-7

First Printing: March 2014

Chapter Illustrations by Gordon Greig
Editorial & Publication Srvs. by Matthias Mayer
Cover Flower Bouquet by Rob Hainer: Shutterstock

Dunbarton North Publications
96 Hillcrest Drive
Toronto, Ontario, Canada
M6G 2E6

God is the perfect poet.

— Robert Browning

Poetry is the breath and finer spirit of all knowledge.

— William Woodsworth

All that is worth remembering in life,

is the poetry of it.

— William Hazlitt

Contents

Conflict

Mortality

Choices

Romance

A Word to the Reader

This modest collection of verse spans many years of writing. The reader will soon discover the author is only a weekend poet who enjoys expressing his thoughts and feelings in something that resembles serious poetry. You might find it odd that he appears to be unaware that modern poetry looks askance at rhyme and meter, those tyrants of unfettered expression. But he embraces without reservation the wisdom of an eminent American poet who has likened the writing of modern verse to playing tennis without a net. Undoubtedly, free verse is a significant and influential development of poetic form but, at its best, it is a companion not a replacement for traditional verse.

In any event, rhyme and meter and rhythm have the advantage of aiding memory and few things in life are more rewarding than remembering a few memorable lines from a good poem. Poetry has a way of living on long after other joys fade. For some, the poetry in this collection will seem rather anodyne, and I agree, but perhaps harmlessness is what we need at present as an antidote to the gratuitous callousness which characterizes so much of our daily experience.

At one time poetry was highly valued as a civilizing force in society. Though this important role has diminished over time, verse still has its unique way of illuminating a wide array of life's special moments as few other media can. The life of an individual as well as the health of a nation are nourished thereby. Poetry cuts through the cant of politicians and humbles in the dust the pretentious. Seasons come and go but a poem endures and stares down untrustworthy fashion.

For Everything a Season covers a wide range of topics and experience. But poetry is essentially spiritual and therefore the underlying theme is what is eternal and unchanging. If in any of the poems in this collection the reader senses the feeling of holiness, then my verse will have served a useful purpose.

The Author
Toronto, 2014

Mea Apologia

I'm not a poet
Just a rhymer
For a poet is a seer
And I can't see
The finer things to me
Are secret
Shrouded in deep mystery
Ah, me,
But still I'll write
Like Dickinson did
And throw the scraps
Into a box and close the lid.

Seasons

Daffodil

Surface Water

A hint of spring is in the air
Surface water is on the run
And in the surreal sky the sun
Seems more like a fond au pair
Than a spinster teacher
Who feels life has passed her by
And lives only to hold each creature
In her frozen stare
That strips all things living bare;
But that's where the au pair comes in
Who never did consider it a sin
To race matchstick boats
Down curbside streams where floats
The echoes of boisterous laughter
And shades of boyhood dreams.
A hint of spring is in the air
Surface water is free at last
And the scent of lilacs
Like perfumed hair
Will soon end earth's Lenten fast.

Springtime

Scilla blossoms blue again
Along the well-worn stone-flagged path
While in small pools left by spring rain
Song sparrows take their bath.

Crocuses pierce the crusty ground
And hyacinth stir from winter's sleep
As jonquils sway without a sound
And ivy on the south wall creeps.

Lilacs spread their scent abroad
Over the stone wall 'cross the way
And dogwood lifts its face to God
As magnolias stoop to pray.

Roses soon will be in bloom
To grace the hour with their display
But this is April, that is June,
So drink the cup of joy today.

A Foreshortened Welcome

Robins, yes, robins, not one
But many (do they fly in flocks)
Brought spring today
To winter's withered stocks.

One on a berry bush, one on a wall
Two on a leafless tree
Another on a rock
And 'neath the rhododendron
Two, maybe, three.

It only took one thoughtless gull
To spoil the welcomed sight;
The robins took their cue from him
And disappeared in flight.

Weather Fashions

Green is now in fashion
I've seen it everywhere
It's become the latest passion
from city hall to Parkman's square
The talk is all about it;
Headlines ring it out
It's bigger than the latest hit
and newsboys shout it out
It's very strange how quickly
fashions turn the page
To think that only yesterday
white was all the rage.

Come with me

Come with me to the garden
The day is cooling and the shadows grow long.
We'll sit on the old stone bench
In the shade of the alder tree
And listen to the cicada's song
And the musings of the bee;
Angels frolic in the laughing fountain
Their encircling wings hover without a sound
And the roses are heavy with scent there
Where their petals sweeten the ground;
The columbine sway in the evening breeze,
The hollyhocks look on with pride
And daisies crowd together with pleasure
As their dark eyes open wide;
We'll stay in the garden until evensong
When the world is hushed in prayer –
There is no place on earth like a garden
For God is always there.

Autumn Voices

Let autumn voices beckon me
And wake my summer's reverie;
Break now Apollo's supine spell
Release the captive, set him free.

Take me down paths I have not known
Where at each bend adventures wait
Among tall birches, crowned with gold,
Unfazed by Midas's solemn fate.

Fill my sight with scarlet delight,
Feast my eyes on cerise and plum,
Send the breeze to tune the trees
And beat and beat the crimson drum.

Set now the smoky hills ablaze
And bathe the streams in dappled light;
Command the clouds to flee the sky
Shrink the day and stretch the night.

And when at last the stage is set
When all the players have their parts
Let voices join in one accord
To hymn the praises of our Lord.

Autumn's Blazonry

A sash of crimson
A splash of red
A glimmer of gold
On maples spread
A touch of amber
A hint of tangerine
A garland of yellow
Among pyramids green
A blush of strawberry
A burst of cerise
A circlet of silver
On each diamond leaf
A necklace of silver
A coronet of sand
A sprinkle of blueberry
In autumn's land.

When I behold the dying of the year
- A Sonnet -

When I behold the dying of the year
And listen for its requiem on the breeze
And summer's green has turned to autumn's gold
And frost has stamped its hallmark on the trees
I remember laughter echoing in the hall
The sound of rushing feet upon the stair
The hiding place beyond the old stonewall
Where golden hours passed without a care
And I remember 'neath the eaves a room
With mullioned windows, ivy-dark, whose light
Fell softly on the saints, their lives, their doom,
Because they believed in holiness, not might.
And so my thoughts return to what is past
Nor would I soon forget old joys that last.

The Cranes

Out of the twilight of the gods
Through air so pure that angels breathe
  and frolic there
On soundless wings that sweep the sky
The sunward-sailing cranes pass by
And lift my soul to heights of joy
That none of earth's delights can bring
Nor teach my fettered heart to sing.

Invincible

Winter came this morning
While we were still asleep.
It came without a warning
On a mantle, wide and deep.
The fence across the pasture
On which I labored long
Forgot the wiles of Nature
And succumbed to Siren's song.
Even the barn that shoulders the hill
And shadows the yard with its length
Forgot to count on Nature's will
And was lulled by its own strength.
The stately pines no longer sing
Their gentlest of songs
But one with one together cling
As the day is swept along.

Visitors

Before they came
I heard their cries
Visitors from across the way;
Each day at dusk it is the same
They fill the pink-tinged skies.
Soon every branch of every tree
Is host to uninvited guests
A tumultuous flock of blue-black birds
Who've stopped for scones and tea.
Maples, chestnuts, beech and oak
Have come alive with feathered folk.

The Challenge

One last fling –
One more chill blast
To freeze the earth
And scatter vague whiteness over all.
One defiant show –
Of many gone before, the last;
Icy fingers of blue
Chilling the back of the weary land:
Zero and snow.

Formless

I walked in the snow the other night
No pattern could I discern;
For shape blended with shape
The sharp and defined were rounded and
smooth
Lines merged and divided and lapsed into
grooves.

Seasons Dead

Bare branches black against a pewter sky
Stir gently in the morning calm;
While on the ground leaves sleeping lie
Like fragments of discarded psalms.

Soon pewter turns to burnished gold
And branches to a weathered gray
And unafraid of winter's cold
Steals from its lair another day.

No requiem through the leafless branches sing
Nor mournful hymn for seasons dead;
While in my mind vague memories cling
To greet the day with watchful dread.

Mystery

Orchid

One

One rocking chair
Where two used to be
One plate, one sweet
One cup of tea;
One open book
Where two used to be
One voice, one thought
One memory;
One pair of shoes
Where two used to be
One life, one path
One certainty;
One beating heart
Where two used to be
One dirge, one grave
One mystery;
One rose, one thorn
One summer flown
One tear, one sigh
One now alone.

The Smile

A wanton smile
On an innocent face
Caught his eye
In the marketplace
And told him something
He was never taught
That good and evil
Though poles apart
Are one and the same
When joined by thought.

The Silent Land

- For Joel -

Come with me to the silent land
Where forests wake without a sound
And rushing streams wash down the sand
To places songless birds are found.

Come with me to the silent land
Where echoes echo soundlessly
And in the park the concert band
Plays music without melody.

Unheard the thunder from the skies
Or rolling surf along the shore
Yet, ever, ever watchful eyes
Which are to silent lands the door.

No voice speaks softly in the night
Nor symphony enchants the day;
No loon's cry greets the early dawn
No church bells toll departing clay.

And yet there is a voice that speaks
More certain than in all things planned
Which lifts the soul to higher peaks
For those who live in silent lands.

Songs from Yesteryear

I hear songs from yesteryear
And wonder where the time has gone
As at my feet leaves, brown and sere,
Lie silent in the paling sun.

No longer are the hours slow
Nor are the summer months like years
And wily seasons come and go
Like children's artificial tears.

Shadows on the path grow long
As sunlight starts its strange decline
And birds that of the night belong
Arise before the moon can shine.

Silence gathers all around
I listen for the tuneful breeze
But Nature does not make a sound
As time itself begins to freeze.

Winter comes, no spring ahead,
For me within that wintry tomb
I see life's flowers lying dead
As stillborn from a weeping womb.

The Intruder

The mist steals in close to the ground
And slips beneath the iron gate.
It glides the path without a sound
Then at the stonewall hesitates.

A moment's pause is all it needs.
It vaults the wall with practiced ease
Then on its way again it speeds
Across the sodden, scattered leaves.

The intruder seems to know the way.
It heads straight for the ivy patch
Which lies outside the window bay
And takes it in a single snatch.

Chrysanthemums with golden globes
Cannot resist this wily thief
Which covers them with ghostly robes
And chuckles at their disbelief.

The roses are the last to fall.
They disappear without a trace
Except for those within the Hall
In a silver vase on Irish lace.

When soon the magic spell's complete
And everything is gone from view
The silent mist curls up, replete,
And waits with stealth for me and you.

Eastward in Eden

I remember a garden
Where a river became three
Eastward in Eden somewhere;
And in the midst of the garden a tree
And the river was clean and clear.
The soil in the garden was good
Eastward in Eden somewhere
And the tree in the middle stood
Heavy with fruit, gold as the sun,
With branches of polished wood
Eastward in Eden somewhere.
And the tree was for instruction
In its leafy crown, a riddle,
Which good, which evil,
Which life, which destruction.
There is a tree in the middle
Eastward in Eden somewhere
Which I have touched, found sweet.
Now angels with their flaming sword
Guard life's slow retreat.

Timeless

And shall we one day comprehend
An unbeginning beginning
And an unending end
When all we've ever known
Are seasons come
And seasons flown
Of life, the present and the past
Of breath, the first and last
Of hours, night and day
Of beauty, blossom and decay
Of love, a song that died
Of sorrow, tears that dried
Of joy, moments turned to ash
Of hope, too late found rash
But when the Master comes
And calls us out of time
Then we'll know, as we are known,
Of the sublime.

Spheres

And can it be
That after thought is through
And reason's run its course
And senses by their vote endorse
The doubt that God exists
And place their bet instead
On nature's random ways;
That some with boldness still insist
That One who is the Word
Spoke spheres to fill the void
While angels, wondering, sang His praise
While angels, worshiping, hymned His praise.

No God

Where is the wise man
Who knows the wisdom of the world,
Who scans the sapphire skies,
Who parses the quivering universe
And through a thousand eyes and ears
Teases out the secrets of the spheres;
Who chases light's headlong flight
Who tracks the galaxies across the night
Who knows where lies the dying star
Who weighs dark matter from afar
Who measures the never-ending space
And marvels at its quickening pace
And yet, and yet, can such a one
Whose mind the infinite has trod
Be, after all, the fool who says, No God.

Unbelief

Death hung in the morning air
Like mist along a sandless shore
Where twisted driftwood, bleached and bare,
Lay scattered with the scars they bore
And phantom gulls in cheerless flocks
Stood silently among the rocks
Which formed a monolithic tomb.
Then, one by one with raucous cry
The gulls rose up into the gloom
And lost themselves in fetid sky
And I, alone, must face the day
Too full of unbelief to pray.

Darkness

How like the night
To steal the light
And leave us, naked and exposed,
To Lethe's pale delight;
Where distant memories shroud
The edge of gloom
And silent shadows sing
Of certain doom.

Conflict

Poppy

Tell it to the dead

Naked aggression, the President said,
(Tell it to the dead)
Of that there is no doubt;
Get them out, force them out,
They can't stay, the President said,
(Tell it to the dead).
It's not about oil, but a new world order,
Is there anything as sacred as a country's border?
Kick some ass, the President said,
(Tell it to the dead).
And we won't negotiate, won't compromise,
Won't back down, won't rationalize.
Read my lips, the President said,
(Tell it to the dead).
One day people will understand,
Remember Poland and the Sudetenland,
Remember Munich and the Alamo
He can't stay, he's got to go,
It's the vision thing, the President said,
(Tell it to the dead)
(Tell it to the dead).

Freedom Square
(For the martyrs of Tiananmen)

Shadows lengthen on that Square
Where hope once flickered in the dark
And youthful voices waged a war
With words that burned like fiery sparks
And just as soon died out;
For other voices, ancient, terrible,
Cried in rage, Let there be Night,
And darkness fell upon that Square
When hope was put to flight.
But still some silent shadows there
Which linger in the spreading gloom
Defy the violent hands that tear
And wait with tears by freedom's tomb.

Ecce Homo

So suddenly he came
A hero of Ogaden
Scudding along on his cardboard shield
A fighting man
(Or was)
With sinewy arms and calloused hands
Instead of legs
To urge him on
With head bent down
A warrior's son
Of Mogadishu town.

The Soldier

Under a sullen springtime sky
A soldier with unseeing eye
Rests against a fallen tree
And wonders why
His comrades died while he lives still
Who led the charge against the hill
Through mud and wire and cannon shell
And fire from the gun from hell
Across the killing fields of No Man's Land
Where one by one his comrades fell.
But with the few he reached the crest
And with grenade wiped out the nest
But could not hold that bloody ground
And so began the grim retreat
Ashamed of yet one more defeat
And so he kneels beside the tree
And wonders why
With sun so high he feels so cold.
For one long moment his vision's keen
Annie and the boys and everything's clean
No mud, no wire, no cannon shells
No blood, no screams, no deathful smells.
Over here, over here, a loud voice cries
While a lark above still bravely flies.

Remembrance

Poppies still grow in Flanders fields
And crosses still stand in rows.
The scars of battle now are healed
Where the tourist comes and goes.

The larks above those fields still fly
They sing an old, familiar song
Unheard by those sent there to die
With comrades, not brave or strong.

The sun still rises, at evening sets,
And darkness brings the watchful moon
While in the shadows lovers fret
Unmindful of those who died too soon.

Church bells ring where guns once roared
With cargoes of malignant death
While frightened men their God implored
To save them from the poisonous breath.

But in the night when all is still
 The place called No Man's Land awakes
And ghosts of Tom and Len and Will
Wander there till morning breaks.

For fallen heroes no more will sleep
To lesser men the torch they threw
Who in their folly did not keep
The promise made to many by the few.

The Gift of Death

They say it came from the sky
God is Great
Gliding, diving, fluttering
God is Great
Like a golden butterfly
God is Great
(An amulet, perhaps)
God is Great
And settled where it lay
God is Great
Where children come to play
God is Great
They say it was a small girl child
God is Great
Who plucked it from its rest
God is Great
And hugged it to her breast
God is Great.

A Song of Hope

Perhaps if I lie very still
The hunter will not find me here
Among the leaves, withered and sere,
The markings of another year.
And perhaps my fur of brown and dun
Will hide me from the hound and gun
And I will see the rising sun
And feel the dew upon my nose
And smell the fragrance of the rose
As run and scamper I through fields;
So when the days of winter's snows
And when the wind of winter blows
I will remember as I dream
Of things that are, and things that seem.

Propaganda

Distant deeds are soon forgotten
Former glories dim with age
Clamorous voices crush the story
Strident voices summon rage.
Weep for unborn generations
Weep for seasons yet to come
Seize the gun or reap destruction
Let the blood stir up the dust
Or see the wheels of commerce rust
And see the hands of progress trussed;
Cry, yes cry, my valiant country
Cry to God, in Whom you trust.
Cry to God, your cause is just
Write your truth on history's page
Let the heathen nations rage.

Mortality

Iris

I am old

I am old, I am old
And my hair's no longer gold
I'm a tale already told
A trail that's grown cold
A shadow long behind
A lode already mined
A shell all cracked and hollow
A field in winter fallow
I am old, I am old
And my days have all been sold.

The Stalker

I have lived with grief so long
That tears no longer flow
And numbness sits where pain belongs
And hours creep so slow.

Death has robbed me of the dreams
That kept my hope alive
And nothing since you died, it seems,
Can make those dreams revive.

Death now stalks, but does not find
Behind that wall of grief
Its willing prey who would not mind
To know sleep's sweet relief.

But time, the torturer, taunts
Me still with maddening delays
While cruel memory nightly haunts
And hounds me all my days.

The Visitor

So soft the rapping at my door
I scarcely knew someone was there
So I hurried not across the floor
And down the twisting, narrow stair.

I wondered with each step I took
Who could this timid caller be
And if he had my home mistook
For someone who lived close to me.

From off my shoulders trailed a shawl
A candle trembled in my hand
Then darkness chilled the shadowed hall
When flame died on the pewter stand.

I put my hand upon the latch
And listened by the shuttered door
Then, unafraid, I raised the catch
And let the shawl slip to the floor.

Gently I pushed the door ajar
And looked into the phantom mist
Which in the pale light from afar
Invited like a lover's kiss.

I did not hesitate to leave
The house had never been a home
I hoped that none behind would grieve
When I was free at last to roam.

O, Death, where is thy sting

The path that leads to the burial ground
Is overgrown with bramble and thorn
As if to say to the travelers there
That death, as life, is a road forlorn.

Nor has the church that stands nearby
From life's duplicity been spared
Through hollow eyes it stares in vain
Across the graves of those who cared.

No longer does the church bell ring
To summon worshipers to prayer;
No longer are there hymns of praise
From pious folk who gathered there.

Even the stones that mark the dead
No longer stand in rows upright
Toppled by weather and decay
They slowly fade from human sight.

Ensnared within a web of weeds
A wingless angel, cast in stone,
Through sightless eyes looks heavenward
Broken, abandoned and alone.

No longer does the iron gate
Keep vagrants from that hallowed place
Who come in search of solitude
While they their shattered lives retrace.

Upon that scene as day departs
The moon its ghastly light bestows
And in the gloom of death's remains
The dead in hope of grace repose.

When roses bloomed

- For Emilie -

She seemed invincible
Back then when roses bloomed
And children loosed from winter wraps
Played hopscotch on the sun-drenched road
While nearby in tall grass the toad
Mused sleepily about its fate
Until a fly, alighting on a swaying blade,
Moved but moved too late.

She seemed invincible
Back then when roses bloomed,
Now winter sings through leafless trees
Her requiem across the seamless snow
So pure, so still, so deep
Where blades of summer grass will grow
And sleeping roses, waiting, weep
And sleeping roses, waiting, weep.

On Dying

I think of dying
Of the worm at the core
Of the night wind rising
Of life's sweet encore.

I think of lightness
Of the spirit set free
Of iridescent brightness
Throughout eternity.

I think of singing
From heaven's golden floor
And silver bells ringing
Forever evermore.

Softly falls the shade of night

Softly falls the shade of night
As from my room the failing light
Steals away to far-off lands
Where soaring gulls sweep golden strands.

Soon the darkness all surrounds
And, one by one, nocturnal sounds
On wings of gossamer intrude
Upon my joyless solitude.

I light a candle to invite
The faithful watchman of the night
And shadows dance upon the wall
As ancient memories come to call.

The moth against the windowpane
Beats and beats and beats again
As whippoorwill through darkening skies
Fills the gloom with mournful cries.

The squeaking bat that shuns the day
Sallies forth in search of prey;
This sightless minister of night
Unerring in its stealthy flight.

Across the way St. Matthew's bell
Weathervane of heaven, hell,
Beckons man to come and pray
At the dying of the day.

Lovers' laughter, painful, sweet,
Rising from the careworn street
Wakens memories of the past
Like blossoms after winter's blast.

The guttering candle fails at last
And with it, hope, the death of past
So here must I with patience wait
For empty days or heaven's gate.

Doomsday

The day put on a sullen face
Like an errant schoolboy in disgrace
Who in dark clouds of speechless rage
Sheds tears upon the textbook page.

Soon all things near turned ashen gray
And I began to rue the day
Not believing it could turn about
The rising wind assured my doubt.

Then suddenly a crack appeared
To put to flight all I had feared;
 A shaft of light broke through the gloom
And swept away my day of doom.

Choices

Daisy

A Disappearing Act

One day I want to disappear
Inside those woods beyond the lake
But those who love me need not fear
For I would not their love forsake.

I want to be where ancient boughs
Hang heavy with their fragrant fruit
Though I would not forget my vows
While listening for the night owl's hoot.

I want to be where silent streams
Glide endlessly through endless days
And dream a thousand vagrant dreams
While wandering woods' labyrinthine ways.

I want to walk that hallowed ground
Far from the rush of city life
And close my ears to strident sounds
And turn my back on civic strife.

When I the pleasures of this world forsake

- A Sonnet -

When I the pleasures of this world forsake
And leave behind what once I thought was best
And critics taunt, he makes a grave mistake
To start a noble but a foolish quest;
I am not searching for that ancient grail
Made holy by the touch of Him who poured
The wine of grace from hand that bore the nail
And then with angel hosts to heaven soared.
And if the compass of my life grows small
And ambition with its godless spawn grows dim
I wait with patience for the Master's call
When with the saints I shall ascend to Him.
So in His steps I bear my daily cross
And count for Him all treasure here as dross.

Lower Ground

Let not the bugle sound
If I should falter on the line
And fail to seize the higher ground
To which all men incline.

Let not the banners wave
If I should take to flight
And seek a coward's forlorn grave
In life's more certain fight.

Let not the drum beat roll
If I should quit the field
And listen to the church bell toll
For those who did not yield.

Song of My Childhood

I remember poplars on a hill
When everything around was still
And nothing moved, not cloud, not breeze
Not cart, not child, not distant seas.

In my mind's eye I saw tall sails
And knew they held a thousand tales
So I listened with my inner ear
To triumphs, tragedies, hopes and fears.

I listened to tunes only sailors know
When they sing at night under moons aglow
And I heard the stamp of dancing feet
And death drums with their mournful beat.

I heard a thousand cannons roar
And the clash of steel on bloodstained floor.
I smelled sweet spices from afar
Mingled with fragrance of salty tar.

Now I remember the poplars still
Though they no longer sail that hill
Swept bare by the carelessness of man
Who must be deaf to the flute of Pan.

The Betrayal

One by one I watched them fall
Thirty silver bits of light.
In vain I tried then to recall
Another time that such a sight
Had met my wondering eyes
But in that moment of delight
My thoughts were filled with wild surmise
About the hours, the days ahead
Of freedom from the hard man's yoke
Of life among the gentler folk
Of fleeing from the coming stroke
Of Roman might and Jewish law
Which sure must fall on Jesus' brow.
No, not for me, the shame, the loss
Not for me the Roman cross
Silver is the truth, the way,
Thirty pieces to betray.

Good Soil

I want to hold in both my hands good soil
And feel its coarseness rub against my skin;
Then through these trembling fingers, worn with toil,
Let it gently cascade back to earth again.

I would not hold it tightly in my grasp
Just tight enough to know it was secure;
Then slowly, slowly, loosening my clasp
I'd watch it slip to earth without demur.

I want to think about the thousand years
It took to change bare rock to living soil;
And hold within my heart those splendid tears
 Which mixed with thousand years of patient moil.

Progress

One day that stand of weathered oak
Which has withstood a hundred years the
  rage of heaven
Yet, undiminished, took each blow, each stroke
And dug itself still deeper with each shock
Until its farthest roots met rock.
Those oak, I say, without intention or ambition
Each reached in girth the size of ten small children
Who, joining hands, danced round them in a ring
And shouted one to the other,
Let us sing,
Let us sing.

Those oak, mute, unknowing, await
  man's intervention
For the sake of progress towards a better life
Which first begins with
  tearing down, leveling, clearing
Then building up with metal, glass or new invention
Until great towers touch with pride the face of God
And lift us up to dazzling heights
While down below in shadowed spaces void of light
Decay with stealth spreads silently at the base
Until all things living slowly disappear
  without a trace.

Romance

Rose

Under a Summer Moon

The moonlight touched the tops of trees
   with fingertips of purest light
Then danced along the dripping eaves
   on silver shoes as soft as night.

Down ivy-covered walls it crept
   and tiptoed past the sculptured swan
But did not stop where willows wept
   along the border of the lawn.

In turn each terrace caught the beam
   where sleeping roses wake to see
What magic had disturbed their dream
   of humming bird and buzzing bee.

While just beyond the glowing stream
   two lovers wrapped in moonlight mist
Are caught by moonlight's silver beam
   Together in a moonlight kiss.

Questions

Is there salt in a tear?
　I know there is in a sigh
For it burns
　Like an August sky.

Is there heat in the blood?
　I know there is in a look
For it bubbles
　Like a molten brook.

Is there fire in the breast?
　I know there is in a touch
But it costs
　Far too much.

Is there sweetness in the heart?
　There was when we kissed
And it spread
　Like a golden mist.

Of Quantity

When it comes to eyes,
I prefer area to perimeter
And as for sighs
Quantity beats quality every time.

Darkness and Depth

I understand that darkness
And depth go hand in hand
And I am sure it must be so
For woods and water never lie
Nor does the eye.

Space Flight

Don't boast of space flight to me
For I have crossed infinity
A dozen times or more
Without such paraphernalia
And science's lore.

First Love

I have known fierce joy
  In the petals of a flower
And ambrosia headier than wine
  In a glowing sunset hour.

I have heard sweet music
  That only the angels know
While listening to the whisper
  Of birch trees in the snow.

I have seen the heavens
  Through blindless eyes alight
And worshipped in the stillness
  Of a holy, starlit night.

I have felt the sea air
  Like a kiss upon the brow
And tasted salt on trembling lips
  That knew not love till now.

When I Awake

When I awake with morning thoughts of you
And dare not look upon the place your head once lay
I chase down corridors of time chance memories
Of when we were together in yesterday;
But phantoms do not please,
　　nor fugitive thoughts delight
And timid ghosts that haunt the day
　　fade in evening light.
Now no touch as soft as dew,
　　no scent of new-washed hair
No quiet morning talks, no laughter on the stair
So I must walk alone throughout the turning years
And live with grief and hide my timeless tears;
But when autumn comes and spreads its golden hue
And autumn mist hangs from the rose
Then I'll remember you.

The Eyes Have It

The other day I traced
  the compass of the heavens
In a glance
  For the heavens aren't really
That immense
  When pupils grow so large
With room enough
  For two heavens, at least,
  Or
Even four.

Awakening

What have you awakened in me?
  Such a gentle, constant longing
Like spring's first sweet breeze
  Over snowdrops thronging.
Will summer's drought and autumn's rain
  And winter's ice
Prove, after all, it was in vain.

Thoughts

You go
And yet you do not really leave
With one of two hearts
Left behind
To fashion each of long, slow days
Loving thoughts
Of you.

And what if

And what if you stopped loving me
Would seasons then elide
Would galaxies collide
Would rain refuse to fall
Would deserts cover all
Would birds refuse to sing
Would bells refuse to ring
Would oceans flee the shore
Would churches close their door
Would love turn into hate
Would evil celebrate
Would clocks stop measuring time
Would climbers cease to climb
Would charity turn to dust
Would hope turn into lust
No, none of these would come to pass
Alas.

Turn Not Away

Turn not away
Your sunlit eyes
From my fierce gaze
Which softens in your love
Though no less ardent
But more true.
Let me look at you
As one who, half-afraid
That vision must deceive,
Drinks from your eyes
Love's sweetness to receive.

Parting

I watched her as she turned and walked away
  with hurried stride;
Her hair no longer golden in the setting sun
  There was nothing more to do or say
All she had left was her pride.
  It was the ending of what had once begun
With hands touching on a windy day
  under a winter sun.
Now all the hours, days, weeks, months and years
Of hopes and fears, of laughter and tears were gone
  As the rising sun dissolves the dawn;
And when that last parting moment passed
  And tearful eyes knew they had seen the last
Of a face in whose every line I read so much
  I remembered still the thrill of that first touch.
Then, looking back just once,
  I turned and walked away
There was nothing more to do or say.

Index of Poems

About the Author

James Greig was born in Toronto, Canada. For many years he taught in the primary and secondary schools of the Toronto (North York) school system. Later, he joined the staff of the Faculty of Education as Professor of Education. Professor Greig was adjunct editor in the school book departments of MacMillan Canada and Ryerson Press where he supervised the production of school textbooks in English Language and Literature. Professor Greig was educated at Queen's University, the University of Toronto and Harvard. He was an international consultant on education with the Commonwealth Secretariat (London), UNESCO (Paris) and the World Bank (Washington). He continues to reside in Toronto.